Cake Ba

Made Easy

Beginner's Guide to Perfect
Cakes, Essential Tips, Delectable
Recipes and Mastering Cake
Icing

Charlotte Powers

Cake Baking Made Easy

Cake Baking Made Easy

Copyright © 2023 by Charlotte Powers

ACKNOWLEDGEMENT

The desire has always been there to compile a cookbook to help broaden knowledge in the aspect of cake baking. From the depths of my heart I want to acknowledge and express my grati- tude to many who helped in making the writing of this book a dream come through.

I want to specially thank Mason Jones for supporting and guiding me throughout the period of writing this book. I can't imagine how far I would have gone without your help.

I also want to thank Evelyn Russell, a Chef and Interior decorator for all the support and assistance rendered.

I acknowledge my wonderful family for showing me much love and support throughout the trying times of writing this book. My dream was made to come through by my family. My profound gratitude also goes to God the giver of life for His mercies and grace.

Contents

INTRODUCTION

Cakes are key elements in celebrating the ceremonies that come from great achievements and turning points in our various lives—these include weddings, birthdays and other festivities to all and sundry, an event or a ceremony such as mentioned above is incomplete not until an elegant cake is placed on the stage. Irrespective of the variety or type of cake, a cake always commands and evokes respect. A beautifully baked and decorated cake is always pleasant to the eyes and to taste.

For many people baking a perfect cake seems like a misery to them, you know that moment when you attend a birthday party or a wedding and you're marveled by the look of the cake and then served a piece of it and you just wish you could take home a larger chunk of it. If you are such an individual faced with the challenge of cake baking, then you just came across the right Book that will change your cake baking story for the better.

It's not a surety or a must that you'll bake a perfect cake at your first attempt, though it may be perfect or it may not. In fact after my first training on cake baking, my first bake wasn't near perfect until I carried out more trials.

Cake baking is a tricky task that needs some skills and proficiency. If the right tools and utensils coupled with the right proportion or amount of materials (measurement) are used by a newbie or starter with the instructions followed, he or she may end up baking a perfect cake. On the other hand an experienced baker may make some major or minor lapses resulting in a baking disaster. In some bakes, the top may be too hard, sometimes the cake overfills the pan or mold (this may result from inaccurate measurements causing some ingredients to be used in excess). The cake may have a basin or hole shape at the top and may also end up being sticky at the center. All these are problems experienced by beginner, regular or amateur bakers which can easily be conquered and then gain more confidence in the cake baking ladder. That's why baking is considered tricky and sometimes complicated.

SOME TERMINOLOGIES IN CAKE BAKING

Baking cakes is a science and an art on its own which accords it a language of its own. So to proceed, you need to get familiar with some of these terminologies:

Bake: to cook by applying dry heat especially in the oven.

Batter: a mixture consisting mainly of egg, flour and milk or water thin enough to pour or drop from a spoon.

Beat: to stir rapidly in order to get an air mix. This can be done with the aid of a spoon, whisk, hand-held mixer or Stand mixer.

Blend: to stir ingredients thoroughly until well Mixed. This can be done using an electric blender.

Caramelize: this is the act of heating a sugar substance until it begins to turn brown.

Combine: to stir different ingredients together until mixed.

Creaming: to beat sugar and butter together to form a light, creamy texture and color. This method helps aerate the batter, thereby helping the leavening process.

Cut In: this is an act of joining butter (or a solid fat) with flour until the fat turns into minute, granular pieces with the resemblance of coarse sand. It can be easily achieved by using two knives in a cross-cutting motion. A special pastry cutter or forks can also be used.

Drizzle: to let a liquid like water fall in minute particles or droplets on top of something.

Dust: to cover the surface of something by sprinkling a light layer of a dry substance like flour, sugar, or cocoa powder.

Fold: the process of gently laying a part of a substance over the other side making an angle of 90 degrees in such a way that the texture is not totally deformed. To do this you need a spatula to fold the bottom of the bowl up and over the top, get the bowl turned 90 degrees, fold again, and repeat the process until complete folding is achieved.

Glaze: to coat with a thick sauce (sugar-based).

Grease: this is the act of rubbing the inside of a baking dish or pan with a fatty substance (especially oil or butter), which serves as a lubricator to prevent sticking thereby making it easy for retrieving the finished cake.

Lukewarm: of a liquid or body being neither hot or cold or slightly warm.

Rolling Boil: hot water boiling with large, fast, and vehement bubbles.

Pan: a baking pan is used for baking (heating foods in an oven).

Softened: a solid substance that has been brought to room temperature in order to make it more flexible.

Soft Peak: this is when egg whites or cream has been beaten to the point at which a peak will bend or slump over to one side when pulled up. To create a soft peak, pull the whisk or beater straight up and out of the mixture.

Stiff Peak: this is when egg whites or cream has been beaten to the point at which a peak will stand erect completely. To create a stiff peak, pull the whisk or beater straight up and out of the mixture.

REQUIRED EQUIPMENT/UTENSILS FOR CAKE BAKING

Making cakes has never been easier or more fun. If you have all of the tools that will be listed stocked in your kitchen then you are more than ready to bake some amazing cakes. If you don't have them, then it's time to get them stocked in your kitchen and start making good use of them. The essential and affordable baking utensils have been listed below

1. Whisk

This is very essential for beating and thorough mixing. There are manual mixers and electronic mixers, and I make use of the manual type because the latter does not come that cheap

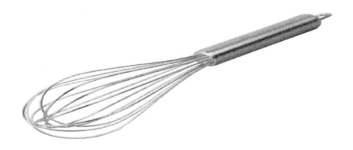

2. Measuring Cups and Spoons

It is a bad practice to underestimate or use random measurements for a teaspoon. It is therefore a wise decision to have a set of measuring cups and spoons to have accurate measurements. They can either be plastic or metal made and come in sets of four or five (1 cup, ¾ cup, ½ cup, ⅓ cup, and ¼ cup). The spoons come in sets of four or five (1 tablespoon, 1 teaspoon, ½ teaspoon, ¼ teaspoon and sometimes ⅛ teaspoon).

3.Hand mixer

While you don't have to go all-out on an extravagant stand mixer or blender, you do require in any event a hand mixer in your weapons store of baking apparatuses. It makes stirring up mixtures and batters a lot simpler and snappier, and it's by a long shot the most ideal approach to blend or mix fixings into a thick, firm treat batter without wearing out your arms because at times you may get stressed out in your arms using a wire whisk.

4. Mixing bowl

They are important especially when you are required to melt and mix butter, milk, chocolate and so on. Having a set of large, medium and small sized mixing bowls to use simultaneously is very important as mostly you may need to make use of more than one mixing bowl. Glass or steel bowls are highly recommended as they're mostly microwave and dishwasher safe. Plastic bowls can retain flavors that you might not want in your muffins, also they are not an alternative when it comes to whisking egg yolks or melting chocolate and sugar over a pot of boiling water. You can further go for bowls with lids in case you need to cover and store some ingredients.

5. Rubber Spatulas

Rubber spatulas are amazing as they have this exceptional ability to conform to the sides of the bowl as you mix and help to get rid of every ounce of your ingredients and incorporate them into the batter. They can last for years upon years if properly cleaned and maintained after each use. Buy a set that usually comes with different sizes of rubber spatulas (small, medium, and large). They can as well be used for other purposes or kitchen activities aside from cake baking.

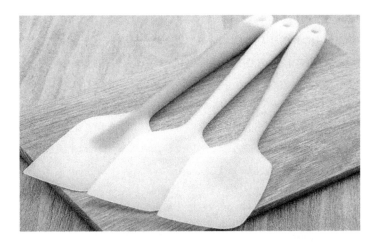

6. Offset spatulas

This is a tool that finds its use mostly during icing. Offset spatulas have a very straight edge that keep the frosting on the sides of your cake straight and nice looking. They are also very useful in spreading batter flat across the pan. It is advisable to get big and small sizes to fit in for different areas of use.

7. Parchment paper

It is placed on the bottom of the pan to aid in easy removal of the cake after baking. If a parchment paper is used on a pan, the tendency of the pan being stained by the cake will be lesser and cleaning will be made much more easier.

8. Pastry brush

The pastry brush has a variety of uses, I bet many don't know this. It is a must have tool for every baker. This is a very ideal tool which can be used to apply grease on a pan before pouring in cake batter.

It is also used to coat cake (glaze) with melted butter or sugar and for painting. It also plays an important role in decoration.

9. Kitchen shears

It is a necessity to always have a special kitchen shear or scissors available for cutting some sachet packaged ingredients and also cutting parchment paper to properly fit into a pan.

10. Cooling rack

The rack provides better air circulation to help hasten up the cooling process. The cooling rack aids proper cooling of the cake after removal from the oven.

11. Oven

The Oven is a very key equipment that contributes greatly to the quality of your cake. A convection Oven is one of the best types of Oven to bake with, it blows hot air throughout the oven as the cake bakes which makes it bake faster and more evenly. Unlike regular ovens that has the heating elements at the top or bottom, the convection Oven helps solve the problem of uneven baking.

12. Kitchen Digital scale

According to a school of thought, measuring by weight is more accurate than measuring by volume. Digital scale also helps to ensure accuracy and precision in measuring ingredients.

13. Plastic Bowl or Bench Scraper

They can be made of either metal or plastic, with plastic being very much suitable for getting bits of batter out of a bowl. The bended side twists to the forms of a bowl, a bowl scraper has no handle like a spatula. Since your hand is nearer to the activity of scrapping, you have more control helping you to get out each and every piece of clingy batter. The level side acts like a dull blade for scooping heaps of prepared ingredients into bowls and pots.

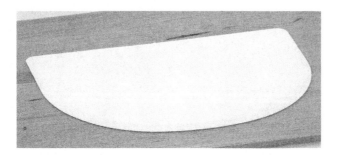

14. Wooden spoon

Wooden spoons also come useful in terms of mixing ingredients. It is strong and can last as long as possible provided it is properly maintained. Never soak a wooden spoon in water, rather wash as soon as possible.

15. Chef's Knife

With this special knife, cutting anything will be no big deal.

16. Sifter or Strainer:

Don't get confused by the name, it's no different from sieves. You wouldn't like an instance when you bite a slice of cake and get a clump of flour or baking soda — sifting can easily prevent such an unpleasant experience. It's probably most useful for sifting dry ingredients or adding a dusting of fine sugar to a finished pan of brownies or cookies. It also comes to use in draining wet ingredients. A sifter is a relatively inexpensive and rather vital piece of equipment, useful in making different cake recipes.

17. Cake Turntable

This is a perfect stand to place your cake for decoration to begin.Having your cake raised when you are decorating is a great advantage. On starting to ice the cake, the capability of spinning the cake while applying the icing will help ensure that there is uniformity and straightness all through. You will also want that cake to be able to spin when you are piping borders round cakes.

18. Pastry Bags and Tips

This is an icing/decorating tool. Pastry bags allow for greater control and more elaborate designs when decorating. As the bag is pressed by hand, icing cream is forced out through the tip and letters and different designs can then be made on the cake. Pastry bags can be reusable or disposable (can only be used once). There are numerous Pastry tips to choose from depending on your desired design.

19. Baking pan

It comes in different types, shapes and sizes. These are a portion of the various sorts of baking pans that each beginner baker or apprentice must have in their kitchen: Square pan, round cake pan, baking pan

(9*13 Inches), Sheet Pan, bundt pan, tube pan, Muffin pan, pie plate pan, loaf pan and Springform pan.

Sheet Pan

Sheet pans are shallow, level baking sheets with a low edge surrounding them. The edge makes it simpler to fix the pan with a parchment paper that won't sneak off it. They're useful for baking sheet cakes, cookies and other flat products.

Sheet pans are accessible in various sizes however the half-sheet (12 x 16 inches) is one of the most adaptable ones to get. Because of the preparing sheets, cleanup of these pans is basic and capacity is in every case simple since they are so light and tiny.

Muffin Pan

This is ideal for preparing muffins and cupcakes and other imaginative cooking thoughts. When appropriately covered in oil and utilized, these pans can be an extraordinary method to make enormous amounts of cakes, biscuits or other finger food.

In view of your inclinations, you can discover muffin pans in various sizes, going from mini to little and medium to enormous and extra-huge Muffin pans.

Tidying up can get muddled which is the reason it is a smart thought to utilize muffin cups or cupcake cups. In the event that you don't have those, make sure to oil the pan appropriately to keep anything from adhering to it after baking.

Loaf Pan

Loaf pans are rectangular shaped pans and are commonly used for baking loaves of bread but can also find its use in cake baking. This is another flexible pan that can be utilized for flavorful and non-cxquisite treats. This is a must have especially for beginner bakers because it has taller sides and expels a great part of the mystery and math involved in choosing a pan that will contain your cake without spilling over the sides.

Bundt Pan

These are pans for cakes where you won't need to include any further adornment. The pan itself has ornamental fluting and has designs on the top and the sides. The final product is a cake that will be adequate to eat, directly as it so happens.

The tubing in the pan makes it adaptable for use with light or thick cakes. It gives an even more even thickness to the whole consideration. Immediately after baking is complete, all you need is some light coating (glaze) sprinkled over the top and your cake is prepared to serve. The only lapses about bundt cake pan is that it is bulky and cleaning up the pan after use is sometimes a major challenge.

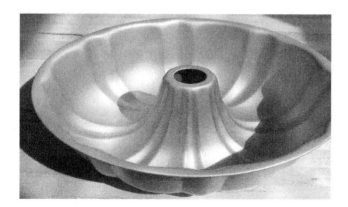

Tube Pan

Due to the striking resemblance with bundt cake pan, countless individuals mistake both for each other. While there is a similitude in their fundamental structure, the tube pan regularly comes up short on the ornamental component that the bundt cake pan offers.

Moreover, tube pans are otherwise called Angel food pans since it is ideal for that cake type. That as well as they work best with light, breezy cakes. The inside container of the pan guarantees that while heating, these cakes get the most help and don't wind up crumbling or having a depressed focus.

Some tube pans may likewise have little feet on the top. This is to enable the cake to be easily cooled upside-down. The feet guarantee that the pan remains upheld and off the counter while putting it upside-down permitting you to get the most entirely delightful cake.

Round Cake Pans (9 inches)

In the event that you prepare as often as possible or normally, round cake pans are an absolute necessity for you. Aside from sheet pans, round cake pans are the most well known baking pan types that you can discover. And they are additionally accessible in various metal sorts.

The shape is perfect since it cooks cake batter uniformly and furthermore helps cool the cakes adequately.

The round cake likewise spares you exertion and time in the process of icing. Accessible in two-pack choices, you can without much of stress cook a stacked or layered cake with the assistance of these. For cooking layers, the 8 and 9-inch choices are the best since they bake the cake layers rapidly.

Be that as it may, when you are getting one, make a point to remember your baking style and flexibility. You can likewise discover sets with three or more distinct sizes of round cake pans, so at any time you can viably make a three-level cake with no issues. In the image below, the second to last stacked pan is 9 inches.

Baking Pan (9 by 13 inches) or rectangular pan

In the event that you need to have a universally handy baking dish, you have to get a baking pan. Baking pans are accessible in an assortment of sizes just as materials. From ceramic and glass to metal and that's just the beginning, picking the correct preparing pan type will descend to your cooking and baking style.

For individuals who like to bake increasingly, an aluminum or clay baking pan is the most ideal alternative. Truth be told, the 9 by 13 size is the ideal one for them as it has higher sides when contrasted with a customary sheet pan and can also be used for other kitchen tasks.

Square cake pan (8-Inch)

Like the 9 by 13 Inches baking pan, this baking pan gets an uncommon notice since it is a smart thought to get a starting point. The 9 by 13 Inches baking pan is progressively rectangular fit as a fiddle and is more qualified for baking huge clusters. Be that as it may, in the event that you need to make smaller clusters, the 8-inch square baking pan will be better for you.

A major benefit or advantage of having this pan (ceramic and glass made) is that it can be transformed into a universally handy baking pan that can be used to make a cake as well as prepare groups of meals, cornbread, and other flavorful food things. And square baking pans are easily accessible due to their prominence so you won't have any issues finding the ideal one you need. The aspect of cleaning up these baking pans is likewise simpler and you are less inclined to confront issues around there.

Pie Plate pan

On the off chance that you're a devotee of pies and love making them, at that point pie plates are an absolute necessity for you. These are shallow baking pans that can likewise be utilized for making brownies, portion cakes, and tarts.

One of the most recognizable highlights of the pan is its scalloped outskirt that can compliment the filling and ensure that you get a delightful pie without fail.

You can discover pie plates in various materials and they each have their own advantages to offer. Metal pie plates accompany a separable base, which implies that you can lift the pan out of it effortlessly.

In any case, clay pie plates are adored in light of the fact that they give the covering a rich, brilliant earthy color outside.

Additionally, individuals likewise like utilizing glass pie plates since they can see the shade of the outside layer and check whether it is prepared or should be cooked for more.

Focus on what you are alright with when selecting a pie plate.

Springform Pans

These are cake pans that can be disassembled. They have a level base, bended and tall sides that fold over the circuit of the base and clasps, which can fix or release the pan sides varying.

Springform pans are ideal for use with cheesecakes, tarts or different kinds of delicate and sodden cakes and treats.

With these pans, the sides can be expelled, which extraordinarily lessens the pressure that delicate cakes may undergo and springform pans make an extraordinary option for pie plates.

TYPES OF CAKES

There are two major types of cakes which are further subdivided into various types/categories. The major types are:

1. Shortened or Butter cake.

2. Foam cake or Unshortened cake.

It is the presence or absence of fat in a cake mixture that determines the type or class it belongs to and how the ingredients are to be mixed together.

1. Shortened or butter cake.

Butter cake is a cake in which the major or dominant ingredient is butter, hence the name. Butter cake is baked with primary ingredients like: butter, flour, sugar, eggs, and leavening agents such as yeast, baking powder and baking soda.

As a matter of fact, if cream butter is mentioned as one of the ingredients required to bake a cake, then consider the cake a type or subcategory of butter cake and it is one of the most popular cakes made in the American soil and the world at large.

A few types or examples of butter cake recipes are: Classic yellow cake, Pound cake, to mention a few.

2. Foam cake or Unshortened cake

Foam cakes are cakes with very little or no fatty ingredients such as butter, shortening or oil. Foam cakes are primarily leavened by the air which is achieved through beating the egg whites contained in them. They are distinct from butter cakes, which contain shortening (source of fat), and baking powder and baking soda for leavening purposes. The egg foaming mixing method used for foam cakes is very different from the creaming mixing method used for butter cakes. In the beating process, the eggs can be beaten separately into three parts, namely; egg white and egg yoke (egg yellow), egg white only, and egg yoke only. The beating depends on the type of cake to be made. Foam cakes are generally springy, light and spongy.

They contain a large percentage of foamed eggs and/or egg whites to a lesser percentage of sugar and small amounts of flour, if used at all. The egg proteins contribute massively to the cellular structure of the cake. Egg foams rule out the prerequisite for adding much flour, leavenings (baking powder and baking soda), and plastic fat (butter, shortening) in these cakes.

Examples of foam cakes are Sponge cake, Angel food cake, Chiffon cake, Genoise cakes, and so on.

ESSENTIAL BAKING TIPS

1. Ensure to be in the right State of mind

This might sound awkward but it really matters. Your current mood before you start the baking process matters a lot and will determine the quality of cake you're ending up with. You will end up making silly mistakes in measuring and mixing and you know an error in the start or foundation can cause some anomalies in the taste and structure of a cake. As a baker, once I'm angry or offended by any one I lay low for a while and bake when I'm more relaxed or in a better mood.

2. Make sure you have time

Time matters a lot, as you cannot be in a hurry and expect to bake a perfect cake. You must take enough time to carry out all necessary procedures required. If a recipe instructs you to bake for 45 minutes and you just decide to do it for 30 minutes, you'll only end up ruining all your efforts.

3. Prepare your utensils/equipments and ingredients

You must ensure that all required equipment is available in your kitchen before you start carrying out any baking procedure. Having the equipment and ingredients you will need to always come handy can make baking a cake a much easier experience.

By doing this you can reduce the tendency of forgetting any ingredients.It will be so unfortunate to be making a good progress only to discover that you have no Whisk or maybe you've run out of baking soda or powder.

4. Go through the recipes

Make sure that you read the entire recipe and comprehend everything in it before you start because even a single step skipped could alter a cake and make it different from a standard cake or a cake that reaches for perfection.

In the recipe, you will be instructed whether or not to preheat the oven and whether or not you should grease the pan. Yes, I know you could be thinking greasing the pan is an all time necessary task. But sometimes you don't need to do that when it comes to baking some types of cakes that need ungreased pans to rise easily. Why hold all that knowledge in your head, alongside with the various objections to each rule when you can just see and follow the recipes.

5. Get good quality ingredients

Various makes of ingredients like butter, yogurt, buttermilk, and flour have different levels of fat, moisture and protein. Little differences can greatly affect the outcome of the final product. This is why it is very necessary to use the makes recommended by the recipe. And don't ever forget to check out for the expiry dates.

6. Temperature of ingredient

You must always use the ingredients at room temperature. So take them out of the fridge first at least 1 hour before using. If a recipe calls for cold butter, melted butter, or room-temperature eggs, remember that any adjustment you make will affect the outcome. The difference between putting a batter with cold butter and one with warm melted butter in the oven, is never the same. It will definitely yield completely different ultimate results.

7. Do not refrigerate your butter

Butter loses moisture the longer it sits in the fridge, which can cause your baked goods to be dry. Buy and use the freshest butter you can find. Check dates on the packing and always select unsalted butter, because salt is a preservative. Meaning salted butter has probably been in cold storage longer than unsalted.

8. Measuring matters

We Americans in the part of estimating are enamored with depending on cups and spoons to give the correct measurements. However good cooks like chefs world wide measure their ingredients by metric weight. The explanation behind this is some flour can change extraordinarily in weight contingent upon the kind of flour, and how pressed it is. Ideally, all home-cooks would utilize scales and metric estimation to safeguard definite measures of wet and dry ingredients. As that is never going to occur, make a point to consistently stir the dry ingredients (flour), spoon in the cup, and Level flour when estimating. Directly scooping without first stirring packs the ingredients down, which means you end up with more than you need. This goes for different ingredients also, yet incorrect measurement of flour is frequently the guilty party in faulty cake bakes.

9. Baking with unsalted butter

On the off chance that you are preparing with unsalted butter, at that point you have full control of the sodium level that will be contained in your cake . On the off chance that you should substitute salted butter, then lessen the extra salt significantly.

10. Climate

Standard "room temperature" is directly around 70 degrees F. In the event that you bake when it's extremely hot outside or severely cold, and the outside temperature is influencing within temperature, your outcomes will be unique. On the off chance that the dampness is higher or lower than ordinary, your outcomes will be unique. That is the reason our grandmothers used to let us know never to heat on a stormy day. The overwhelming dampness noticeable all around impacts the capacity of the batter to rise and dry.

11. Ensure using fresh ingredients

Leavening agents like yeast, baking powder and baking soda, lose much of their effectiveness after six months or so, meaning your baked goods won't rise the way they should. So just like I do, I suggest you buy a new yeast or baking powder every 6 months and dispose the old ones.

12. Scrape the bowl

This is very crucial especially when using a standing mixer. Recipes often remind you to do this, but in the case of mixing batter in a standing mixer, you're trying to mix the ingredients together as thoroughly as possible, but not all parts of the mixture like butter, eggs, or sugar the will be properly mixed as some portions would be stuck to the bottom and sides of the bowl. The remedy to this is stopping the mixer every 30 seconds or more and scraping the mixing bowl. However, make use of a rubber or flexible spatula or bowl scraper to fit into the sides of the bowl.

13. Grease and dust your cake pan

Your cake pan ought to be consistently greased/lubed and dusted with flour, so the cakes can sneak out of the container effectively subsequent to cooling. In the event of utilizing a bundt pan, the more sections your bundt cake container has, the more you have to focus during the lubing and dusting process. I like to utilize a baking spray like Baker's Joy that consolidates flour in the splash, so I get the advantage of greasing and dusting at the same time.

14. Oil and sugar

For an extra dried up outside, have a go at lubing and sugaring the pans. This gives cakes a firm sweetened external layer. Oil the pan well, at that point hurl sugar in the pan to totally cover the sides.

15. Applying nonstick splash

When splashing pans with nonstick spray, hold the pan over the sink (to decrease tidy up) and shower each niche and crevice.

16. Isolating Eggs

The most ideal approach to isolate eggs for heating is to start with cold eggs, crack them on the counter (splitting on the bowl will in general make progressively broken pieces), strain out the yolk through your fingers and spot in independent dishes. Evacuate any shell trash with a fork.

17. Rapid warming of eggs

To carry eggs to room temperature rapidly, split them into a few little dishes before beginning the activity of mixing the ingredients. On the off chance that you are in a gigantic rush, run them under warm faucet water for 5 minutes before breaking.

18. Reviving flavors

Flavors lose their power after some time. Ever open a container of cinnamon and wonder where the fragrant smell went? To revive flavors for preparing, place them in a dry skillet and set over medium warmth. Watch intently. The second you can smell the flavors, hurl and expel from heat. This attracts the rest of the oils to the surface so you can utilize the remainder of your zest container.

19. Cooling

Chill cakes upside off on a cooling rack. This will level out the tops, making simple to-stack circles for layer cakes.

20. Replacements

Don't be too quick to put the blame of your cake woes on the recipe you utilized for a baking project, however on the off chance that you've left a negative remark on some other site related to replacements and bombed plans, I'm conversing with you. Substitute at Your Own Risk. Actually, there's no genuine substitute for white granulated sugar, white wheat flour, or genuine butter. You most certainly can substitute all you need, yet don't be disturbed if your cake doesn't turn out as appeared in photographs. Particularly when replacing sound ingredients. Cakes are brilliant desserts which are intended to be nice treats, and nice treats are intended to be delighted in with some restraint.

21. Do not readjust the oven temperature and cooking time for quicker baking

Cakes particularly lose dampness when cooked with too high temperature, and you additionally risk consuming fragile fixings.

22. Keep the Oven Closed

It's enticing to glimpse inside to perceive how things are going, however it's simply not a smart thought. In case you're preparing a cake, the inundation of air, or even the vibration of the stove entryway, can make it fall. Also, you let all the warmth out, which is clearly going to influence the heating.

23. Prepare in the inside

Position the pans as near the focal point of the oven as could reasonably be expected, except if in any case noted in your recipe. They shouldn't contact one another or the oven dividers. In the event that your oven isn't sufficiently wide to put pans one next to the other, place them on various racks and somewhat counterbalance, to consider air dissemination.

24. Brisk cool

At times we're in a rush and need our cake to cool (or chocolate to set) so we can complete our recipe. In such a case, place the prepared products in the cooler for 20-30 minutes, or in the cooler for 10-15 minutes to cut the temperature down. Try not to disregard them.

25. Convection is better

In the event that you live in a more up to date house/loft, odds are you have an oven with both regular and convection heat. Convection heat offers a more prominent wind stream and drying while at the same time preparing, making higher crustier, prepared merchandise. So when would it be advisable for you to utilize convection? I like to utilize convection on treats and breads since it will in general make more full treats with a fresh outside and delicate focus.

26. Make preheating a priority

It's so enticing to toss a pan of brownies into the broiler before your oven arrives at the predetermined temperature, but don't do it! Baking is a science, recollect? The temperature will profoundly impact the result.

27. Cool before icing

Tolerance is a goodness throughout everyday life and baking. Never ice a cake, cupcakes, or treats until they have completely cooled, except if you like icing that slides out of the way.

28. Preheat changes

At the point when you realize you will have your oven entryway open for longer than typical (You are stacking something overwhelming or fragile into the oven. Or on the other hand setting numerous heating sheets in the oven). I preheat the oven to 25 degrees higher than suggested, at that point bring down the temperature as coordinated, when I close the oven entryway. That way, my prepared products are bound to begin at the correct temperature. Simply remember to bring down the heat back to normal.

29. Streak freeze

Streak freezing is the way toward freezing something opened up, so you can later wrap and freeze it without upsetting its appearance. I do this with iced cakes and cupcakes regularly. Spot them in the cooler revealed for 30-an hour, until the outside is hard, at that point wrap well and freeze. At the point when you are prepared to utilize the cake, open up first, at that point defrost for a few hours on the ledge.

30. Blend all together

Butter and sugar ought to quite often be beaten together before including whatever else. Dry ingredients ought to be joined together altogether in one bowl before including fluids. Fluid ingredients ought to consistently be included after the initial two stages are finished. This strategy makes smooth in any event, blending.

31.Bake ahead of time

As an efficient device, you can make pie outside layers and treats ahead of time, at that point freeze and prepare directly from the cooler. Additionally attempt streak freezing (above) to complete your prepared products days before an occasion. This diminishes the pressure of gathering and arranging.

32. Baking with chocolate.

When adding softened chocolate to a formula, recall you are including additional thickness and fat. On the off chance that you are making the formula without any preparation, make sure to utilize somewhat less fat (oil or margarine) than you regularly would, and there should be an increment in raising operators (leaveners).

33. Avoid overbeating or underbeating the batter.

Underbeating or overbeating will influence the surface and volume of the cake. Most plans are tried utilizing an electric blender, which creates the most noteworthy volume. Peruse the recipe to be certain which strategy to utilize, electric or hand blending. One moment of medium beating time with a blender approaches, for the most part rises to around 150-180 strokes by hand.

34. Creaming butter and sugar.

This is an exceptionally significant preparing step that individuals like to hold back on. Creaming butter and sugar implies beating it at rapid speed with an electric blender until the butter is cushioned and the sugar separates. Skirting this progression impacts the light vaporous nature of your cake. I suggest creaming for 3-5 minutes. In the event that you don't ordinarily do this, you will see a distinction in your treats and cakes right away.

35. Fill Cake Pans Only 2/3 Full

While it may be enticing to fill a cake dish right to the top before placing it into the broiler, fight the temptation. Filling it to around 2/3 full will permit the hitter to grow and ascend, without flooding over the edge of the container. In case you're left with an additional batter, don't stress! There are a wide range of one of a kind approaches to repurpose extra batter.

You could possibly get an extra pan or distribute to cupcakes pans.

36. Go for quality bakeware

I like to bake in clay heating dishes and pie pans since they offer steady heating. For cake pans, select metal straight edged pans that are thick and tough.

37. Is your butter running out?

You can never have a lot of butter close by, as I would see it. On the off chance that you begin preparing and happen to come up short on margarine, measure the proper measure of canola oil or shortening. It doesn't offer a similar rich flavor, yet won't irritate your formula. You can even have a go at subbing crushed avocado for the spread!

38. Why cracked cakes?

It can depend on the oven being too powerful, each cook knows his or her oven well. And yes! Experiences are made by making attempts. In that case, lower the temperature during cooking. It can depend on the leavening if it tends to crack too much. Always calculate that every 500 grams of flour needs a sachet of chemical leavening for sweets.

39. Over dense and compacted cake

If the cake is too dense, compact, it means that you have not added enough whipped egg whites and yolks. The butter was cold, and cooked at too low a temperature. If you work the ingredients a little, the mass cannot bind, and a compact dessert is created.

40. Too dried cake

If the cake is too dry it usually depends on the high temperature and prolonged cooking. It may also be as a result of a little sugar being added into the batter. To avoid a problem such as this, always ensure enough sugar is added into the batter.

41. Does the cake deflate?

It depends on the temperature of the oven, if a too high crust is formed, and under it it is raw.

If it deflates after cooking, it means that the cake is still raw inside, and probably because you cooked it at too high a temperature. Either you immediately take the cake out of the oven, or you immediately turn out the cake. As a matter of fact desserts hate temperature changes!

42. Issues with sticking to pan

Spot a thick, clean towel in the kitchen sink and pour a pot of bubbling high temp water over the towel to warm it (don't plug the sink to hold the water, permit it to deplete out). Set the dish on the hot towel and leave it for a moment or two, the cake should end up being without any problem.

Turn the dish over on a sheet of wax paper or a cooling rack. Spot a perfect, meager cotton towel on top and utilizing a hot steam iron, heat the base for a couple of moments. The pan should lift off neatly.

Cool cakes totally in the dish before attempting to expel them. Try not to cool inside the oven where there's warmth, they're best cooled on a rack put on the counter. Tenderly dip a blade between the outside of the cake and within the pan. Run it along the edges to relax things up before turning over.

43. Don't overbake

This may appear glaringly evident, however numerous bakers think their prepared merchandise are not exactly done, just to haul them out after they're over the hill. Continuously set the chance to the base preparing temperature, at that point check. Treats are generally best when you haul them out just marginally half-cooked in the middle.

Continuing to cook after the stipulated time as mentioned in the recipe is not a good idea.

44. Never store warm

Continuously, consistently cool your baked cakes to room temperature before wrapping or covering them. The dissipation and buildup from warm cakes, wrapped too early, can demolish the brilliant fresh tops.

45. Use cooled sheet pans

As a baker, you'll be prompted to try out different things just like academics embark on different research every now and then. In the case of using sheet pans, ensure to cool between batches before reusing. Wipe the outside of each with a paper towel, or line with another sheet of material paper.

46. More hints on chocolate

The best chocolate contains just cocoa butter and no different fats. Understand names. In the event that the chocolate contains vegetable oils, pick something different.

47. Yeast

If you can bake with yeast as your leavener, refrigerating dry active yeast helps in preserving it and retaining its lifting power.

48. Freezer stockpiling

Here are baking ingredients you can keep in the cooler to build their life expectancy: baking powder and soda, flour (all assortments), nuts, berries, flavors, buttermilk, ready bananas, and additional butter. Simply ensure your baking soda and other canned or container ingredients are properly covered or placed in an impenetrable compartment to avoid ingesting undesirable scents for each.

49. Baking Soda and Baking Powder

Recipes with both baking soda and baking powder are very common. Ever wonder why? Both are utilized to kill the ph equalization of a formula and offer a vaporous lift. Nonetheless, on the off chance that you simply include baking soda, you may make balance, however not lift. Baking soda needs some corrosive (acid) to respond. You could utilize baking powder alone, however then your completed dessert treats may taste excessively acidic. A mix of both is generally the best and most logical option.

50. Commit some baking reciprocals into memory

Though there's always the need to have a measurement and conversion chart which you will find in the last chapter of this book, nevertheless it is very good to know these basic reciprocals.

3 teaspoons = 1 tablespoon. 4 tablespoons = ¼ cup. 5 tablespoons + 1 teaspoon = ⅓ cup, 2 cups = 1 pint, 2 pints = 1 quart, 4 quarts = 1 gallon.

51. Refreshing flavors

Flavors lose their force after some time. Ever open a container of cinnamon and wonder where the fragrant smell went? To invigorate flavors for preparing, place them in a dry skillet and set over medium warmth. Watch intently. The second you can smell the flavors, hurl and expel from heat. This attracts the rest of the oils to the surface so you can utilize the remainder of your flavor.

52. Salt for baking

There are relatively few things I get inflated over, however salt is one of only a handful. I don't purchase essential iodized table salt. On the off chance that you test-taste table salt with quality ocean salt you will see an unmistakable distinction in flavor. This little change helps through in heated products. Continuously pick fine-grade quality salt for heating, over amount.

53. When to filter

At the point when a formula calls for filtering, measure first, at that point filter. I filter just when making ultra light cakes or scones, and while fusing cocoa powder into other dry fixings.

54. Dairy replacements

Be that as it may, subbing skim for entire milk can have an appalling impact. On the off chance that a formula calls for entire milk and you just have skim, include 2 tablespoons of softened butter.

55. Cutting your cake

On the off chance that your cake is cold, utilize a hot blade. (Run it under boiling water and wipe it dry.) If your cake is hot, utilize a chilled blade (place in the cooler for a couple of moments) and work quickly. For clean cuts, wipe the blade with a wet paper towel between each cut.

56. Folding

Sometimes a recipe may require you to carry out folding. While rotating the bowl, from the bottom sweep the spatula all the way up to the top to combine the new ingredient gradually into the batter.

57. Don't have a cooling rack?

If you do not have a cooling rack you can make use of the parchment paper you used for baking. Slide it straightforwardly onto the cool counter. On the off chance that you have to retain oil, slide the prepared products onto leveled paper food item sacks to cool.

58. Stay supplied with baking specials

For baking spontaneously, I like to keep these things close by: baking powder, baking soda, flour (all purpose), granulated sugar, earthy colored or brown sugar, nectar, dry dynamic yeast, quality salt, unsalted butter, coconut oil, cocoa powder, different flavors, unadulterated vanilla concentrate, destroyed coconut and nuts. A great deal of baking enchantment can occur when they're in place.

59. Knowing cake servings

It's difficult to quantify servings for pan sizes, particularly when anxious youths are cutting their own bit of cake! However, here are some standard rules: 8 inch square cake = 6-8 servings, 8 inch round layer cake = 12-16 servings, 9 by 13 inch sheet cake = 12-16 servings, 12-cup bundt cake = 12-20 servings.

60. Sugar levels

When changing sugar in a formula, be cautious. An excessive amount of sugar can cause a dull outside layer. Too little can cause excess lightness on an outside layer, or extreme surface.

61. Layer by layer

For preparing equitably baked cakes, without adjusted tops, bake layer-by-layer. To do this, utilize 3 of a similar size/shape of pans, and prepare in 3 separate batches and place them on top of each other.

62. Making your own buttermilk

At the point when a formula calls for buttermilk, after all other options have been exhausted, you can make your own! Measure one cup of entire milk, halting near the top. At that point include 1 tablespoon lemon squeeze or rice vinegar, to level off the measuring cup. Permit the milk to sit for 10 minutes and turn sour. At that point use as is required.

63. Cake flour replacement

On the off chance that a formula calls for cake flour, when absolutely necessary, you can substitute generally useful flour + corn starch. Measure 1 cup of flour. Expel 2 tablespoons of the flour and spot back taken care of. At that point top the measuring cup with 2 tablespoons of cornstarch and sift properly.

64. An attractive completion

For an overly proficient looking cake, give your iced cake a polished completion. Utilize a hair-dryer on medium warmth over the outside of the cake directly before serving, so it sparkles.

65. Cutting bars

Line the heating pan with material paper or foil before preparing. When the bars are cool, lift the entire sheet out of the pan from the corners, and strip back the paper. At that point score the edges, so your pieces are equitably estimated. Chop straight down, and pull in reverse, moving the blade all over like a saw, as you expel it. Wipe the blade before making the following cut.

66. Icing a cake

Dismiss the overabundance pieces off the cake and freeze each layer for simple stacking. At that point utilize a long icing spatula to spread the icing on equally. Turn the cake while icing. A rotating cake table proves to be useful here.

67. Filling Pastry bags

To handily fill pastry bags, place the pastry tip clinched and secure it with a coupler ring set. At that point place the tip of the channeling pack down into a tall drinking glass. Overlap the edges of the pack over the glass to keep the sack open while filling.

68. Pastry icing

 On the off chance that you are new to Pastry icing, purchase a lot of Pastry tips with a few standard sizes (no compelling reason to go over the edge) and practice on a bit of wax paper before applying icing onto your cake using the pastry bag. The rear of the bundle will have a few aides regarding what shapes you can make with the tips you purchased.

69. Toothpick/Skewer Test

On the off chance that you love baking cakes, it's probably a smart thought to put resources into a bundle of long toothpicks or wooden sticks for testing because ordinary toothpicks simply don't slice it when you have to test a deep cake. After heating, embed a long wooden stick into the inside most part of the cake. On the off chance that it confesses all (comes out clean), turn off the oven and cool the cake on the counter. Otherwise keep heating.

70. Different approaches to realize your cake is done

In the event that you don't have toothpicks or sticks close by, you'll realize your cake is completely heated when: the sides pull away from the pan, the cake is pillowy and brilliant on top, the top skips back when you contact it, as well as when the inner temp peruses 210 degrees Fahrenheit on a thermometer.

How to Grease and line your cake pan

Greasing and lining a baking pan is an operation that can be useful in many sweet and savory recipes! By greasing the pan properly you will get perfectly smooth and defined cakes and pies; moreover you will allow your preparations not to stick to the baking pan, making it even easier to unmold them.

To Grease and line a baking pan, you will need: a cooking spray with flour, parchment paper, softened butter, a pencil, a brush, scissors and a ruler and follow the steps outlined below.

1. Tear a square of parchment paper (or a bit of paper towel after all other options have been exhausted): Put a liberal touch of oil (Grease) on one side and take a few to get back some composure on the contrary side, keeping your hand clean. Smear oil over every last trace of within the pan: the base, sides and corners. Be liberal!

In case you're utilizing a spray, this progression is basic: just generously spray everywhere throughout the pan. On the off chance that you have a spray with flour in it, you can skirt ahead to No. 3.

2. Flour or Dust the pan: Flour will adhere to the oil including an additional layer of security among pan and cake. Flouring is fulfilling yet it can get untidy; we propose wearing a cover and working over the sink.

Take a spoonful of flour and hold it uniformly over the pan. Shake your wrist to send the flour showering down into the pan. It most likely won't scatter uniformly now; don't stress. Take the pan over to your sink and tilt it to and fro, arriving in a desperate predicament or sides varying to stir up floats of flour and send them to sparser territories. When your pan looks about equitably secured, flip around or turn upside down and delicately wrap the base to shake out any abundance of flour.

3. Lining the pan with parchment paper is a stage that can feel pointless after you've lubed it as of now. Yet, trust me, it's justified, despite all the trouble.

(Note: Some plans call for just lubing (greasing) and flouring a pan, while some call for greasing and lining with parchment. You can follow your formula, or do the entirety of the procedures outlined here to be extra certain your cake won't stick.)

- Place the cake pan or baking tray on the baking paper and trace the perimeter of the outer edge with a pencil.
- then cut it out with scissors.
- Now prepare the parchment paper to coat the edge of the cake pan: measure its height.
- Transfer the measured height to the parchment paper with pencil marks.
- Then cut strips and place into the pan and you're good to go.

PROCEDURES IN CAKE MAKING

1. Get all required ingredients prepared.

In cake making, as in the planning of different dishes, an efficient arrangement must be followed if acceptable outcomes are wanted. As a baker, there's no way you'll hope to have a fruitful cake on the off chance that you need to quit during mixing to get a portion of the ingredients or on the other hand a portion of the utensils prepared. Before you start mixing, all the utensils and ingredients ought to be gathered and any of them that require exceptional planning ought to be arranged. At that point, if the recipe is right, if the ingredients are estimated precisely and consolidated accurately, and if the preparation is done appropriately, you are sure to achieve your goals of success in cake making.

The primary action item, when a cake is to be made, is to peruse the recipe or formula which will be given in this book for different types of cakes in order to decide exactly what is required and to see if all the ingredients called for are available. With this done, all the utensils ought to be set advantageously on the table and the ingredients gathered and estimated. A few specialists educate the utilization of weighing concerning the ingredients in cake since weight is constantly viewed as increasingly exact than measure. On the off chance that a recipe calls for weighing, it will be found simpler to utilize the given instruction to weigh than to attempt the use of ordinary measurement; be that as it may, when a formula requires measurement, and doesn't state weighing, it is indiscreet to endeavor to utilize digital balance for estimating or measurement.

The estimating of the fat regularly requires a little consideration. For example, if just 1/4 cup of butter or some other fat is required, it might be progressively more helpful to quantify it with a tablespoon than with a cup. Something else, except if the recipe calls for softened fat, the fat ought to be estimated by squeezing it down close into the cup until it arrives at the imprint demonstrating the necessary sum. In the event that the fat is hard and cold, as is generally the situation when it is first taken from the fridge, it will be hard to cream. A decent arrangement is to let the fat remain until it is 70 degrees Fahrenheit, or conventional room temperature, before the blending is begun.

The dry ingredients utilized in cakes incorporate the sugar, flour, baking powder, flavors, and so forth. Granulated sugar only occasionally requires any arrangement with the exception of estimating. In any case, sugar other than granulated, especially brown or earthy colored sugar and pummeled sugar, ought to be moved with a moving pin and afterward filtered so as to liberate it from any protuberances it may contain. Flour ought to be filtered once before estimating and again with the baking powder, or soda and cream of tartar, and salt all together to blend them. Other dry ingredients, for example, flavors and once in a while pummeled sugar, may likewise be filtered with the flour and other dry ingredients. On the off chance that the dry raising specialist (dry leavening agent) has all the earmarks of being uneven when the spread is expelled from the can, it ought to be worked smooth with a spoon and filtered before it is estimated. A little work wire sifter might be utilized for this reason.

The fluid ought to be estimated by emptying it into the estimating cup with the cup fixed and level. The eggs, which are, obviously, one of the fluid ingredients, ought to be neither broken until not long before they are to be utilized, nor beaten until the blend is brought to where the eggs are to be included. On the off chance that the whites are to be utilized for the planning of icing after the cake is baked, they ought to be kept in a cool spot until they are beaten.

Organic products, nuts, and different incidental ingredients ought to be set up before the mixing of the cake is started; that is, they ought to be purified, cut, ground, or hacked, as the case might be, with the goal that it won't be important to stop the mixing of the cake to do any of this work. In the event that they are to be dug with flour, this might be done at the time they are prepared.

2. Get the baking pan ready.

For the baking pan, it depends on the type of cake you want to make. It is a necessity that the pan is made ready for use before mixing is started. If baking a regular butter cake or any other butter related cake, the pan must be adequately greased just as it has been earlier outlined above. The fat intended to be used to grease or oil pans of any sort ought to be a perfect, dull fat. Less will be required to cover the surface of the pan if an oil instead of a butter is utilized. In the event that butter is chosen for this reason, it should initially be liquefied and afterward left to form until the clear fat that ascents to the top can be assembled. Although, fats that are more affordable than butter are completely acceptable. For lubing pans, thus butter ought not be utilized except if different fats are not available. But foam cakes like the Sponge cake should never have their pans greased as it is a surety that acceptable results will certainly be gotten by putting them in a bare pan. For sponge cakes the highest treatment you can come up with is flouring the pan.

CAKE RECIPES

Going into baking proper, we'll first look at how a regular butter and foam cake is prepared then treat as many other types as possible.

BUTTER CAKE

Preparation Time: 10 minutes

Cook Time: 50 minutes

Total Time: 1 hour

INGREDIENTS

- 7 oz flour or cake flour (1½ cups)
- 1 teaspoon baking powder
- ½ teaspoon salt
- 1 teaspoon vanilla extract
- 4 tablespoons full cream milk
- 225 g butter unsalted butter, at room temperature.
- 7 oz sugar (200 g)
- 4 enormous eggs

INSTRUCTIONS

1. Preheat the oven to 375°F (190°C).

2. Grease the pan (8x8-inch or 9x9-inch square pan, round pan) with some butter.

3. Mix the flour and the baking powder together and sift. Add the salt and mix properly and put aside the mixture.

4. Using a hand mixer, beat the butter and sugar until well incorporated or pale yellow in color, this should take about 3 to 5 minutes.

5. Add the eggs one after the other with not more than 2 minutes of beating each until the mixture turns creamy.

6. Using a rubber spatula, scrape down the sides of the bowl for thorough mixing.

7. Add in the vanilla extract and mix properly.

8. Bring in the flour mixture and mix well and add in the full cream milk

9. Pour the batter into the greased baking pan and distribute evenly and shaking it a bit

10. Bake until golden brown and cooked, about 40 - 50 minutes.

11. You can spread aluminum foil on the top after it is set to prevent over browning of the cake top.

12. After about 50 minutes use a toothpick or tester to test for doneness.

13. Retrieve the cake from the oven after it must have cooled and let it cool properly on the cooling rack. And your cake is ready to be cutted into pieces and served.

SPONGE CAKE

Preparation Time: 20 minutes

Cook Time: 30 minutes

Total Time: 50 minutes

Servings: 12

INGREDIENTS

- 4 enormous eggs
- 1 cupful all purpose flour
- 1½ cups powdered sugar or 1 cup granulated sugar
- 3 tablespoons melted butter
- 2 tablespoons hot water
- 1 teaspoon baking powder
- 1 tablespoon vanilla extract

INSTRUCTIONS

1. Preheat the oven to 350°F.

2. Whip 4 eggs in a bowl using a hand or stand mixer on high speed for about 1 minute.

3. Add the powdered sugar (or 1 cup of granulated sugar) in thirds while whipping.

4. Get an 8 inch round cake pan lined with aluminum foil and spray with a nonstick spray.

5. Pour the melted butter and hot water in a separate bowl and whisk together to mix.

6. Whip the eggs and sugar for about 10 minutes. This is done so that the cake can rise properly.

7. Add 1 tablespoon of vanilla extract.

8. Now add the flour into the whipped eggs and fold them carefully with a spatula. Ensure not to overfold or the cake will be tough. The folding is just to incorporate the flour.

9. Bring in the melted butter mixture into the batter and carefully fold with a spatula until no streaks of liquid are visible.

10. Pour the batter into an 8 inch round cake pan or the one you have available.

11. Place gently inside the oven and bake for about 30 minutes on the middle rack of the oven.

12. Check the cake for doneness with a toothpick/skewer by inserting it in the middle. If it

comes out clean without crumbs on it, the cake is ready to be removed from the oven.

13. Then invert it onto a cooling rack and remove the foil. Allow to completely cool before serving or icing.

ANGEL FOOD CAKE

Preparation time: 20 minutes

Cook time: 45 minutes

Total time: 65 minutes

Yield: 10 servings

INGREDIENTS

- 12 egg whites
- 1 cup (130 g) cake flour
- 1 cup (115 g) powdered sugar
- ¾ cup (180 g) granulated sugar
- 2 teaspoons vanilla extract
- 1½ teaspoons cream of tartar
- ½ teaspoon table salt
- ½ teaspoon almond extract

Special equipment:

Angel food/tube cake pan

INSTRUCTIONS

1. Preheat the oven to 325°F.

2. Add egg whites into a bowl and beat with a hand or stand mixer until it becomes frothy which takes about a minute.

3. Add cream of tartar, powdered sugar, salt, and the vanilla and almond extracts into the egg white bowl and turn on the mixer until stiff peaks are formed.

3. Sift the cake flour Combine the cake flour into a bowl or a piece of parchment paper.

4. Gently combine the egg whites with the dry ingredients.

5. Pour the batter into an ungreased 10 inch angel food cake pan. Place in the oven and bake for 40 minutes. The top should be springy, dry, golden, and slightly cracked when done and the cake springs back when lightly pressed.

6. Cool the cake inverted. Complete cooling must be achieved with the cake still in the pan for 90 minutes. You must be patient enough if you do not want your cake to collapse.

7. When the cake pan is totally cool to the touch and you've quietly held up or waited an hour and a half, slide a blade around the edges and the middle

cylinder. Flip around it. Expel the base from the sides. The cake will at present be appended to the base. Slide a blade between the base and the cake.

ORANGE BUNDT CAKE

Preparation Time: 10 minutes

Cook Time: 1 hour

Total Time: 1 hour 10 minutes

INGREDIENTS

- 3 cups flour
- 1½ teaspoons baking powder
- 1 teaspoon salt
- 2 cups sugar
- 1 cup vegetable oil
- 4 large eggs
- ½ cup orange juice
- 1 teaspoon vanilla extract
- 1 teaspoon grated orange zest
- 1 cup buttermilk

For the glaze

- 1 cup icing sugar
- 1 tablespoon of orange juice
- 1 teaspoon grated orange zest

INSTRUCTIONS

1. Preheat the oven to 350°F.

2. Lubricate the bundt cake pan and set aside.

3. Combine flour, baking powder, salt in a bowl, whisk and set aside.

4. Beat sugar and butter together in a large bowl and eggs one at a time until mixed.

5. Add orange juice, vanilla extract, orange zest to the egg mixture until mixed.

6. Combine the flour and buttermilk mixture in a large bowl and beat until mixed properly, combine with the egg mix and pour the batter into the lubed bundt cake pan and place it in the preheated oven.

7. Bake from 50 minutes to 1 hour or until a toothpick inserted into the pie comes out clean.

8. Remove from the oven and cool in the pan for 15 minutes. Remove and allow to cool completely on a rack.

For the glaze

Mix the powdered sugar, orange juice and zest and beat to combine and pour on the chilled cake.

POUND CAKE

Preparation Time: 10 minutes

COOK TIME: 60 minutes

Total Time: 70 minutes

INGREDIENTS

- 9 enormous eggs
- 3 ¼ cups all-purpose flour
- 2 cups sugar
- 2 cups softened salted butter

Note; each ingredient is usually made equivalent to one pound.

INSTRUCTIONS

1. Preheat the oven to 325°F.

2. Coat a 10-inch bundt cake pan generously with nonstick spray or apply butter as grease and put in a safe spot.

3. Utilizing a hand or stand mixer, combine the butter and sugar for 2 minutes until light and soft.

4. Include the eggs, each in turn, blending until joined, scratching the sides with a rubber spatula at different intervals.

5. Turn the mixer to low and include the flour gradually until joined, again scratching the sides with the spatula to guarantee everything is consolidated uniformly.

6. Pour the batter into the prepared pan and heat for an hour, or until a blade or long toothpick embedded comes out clean.

7. Permit the cake to cool in the pan for around 20 minutes and afterward discharge onto a cooling rack to cool totally.

CHIFFON CAKE

Preparation Time: 15 minutes

Cook Time: 45 minutes

Total Time: 1 hour

INGREDIENTS

- 2 cups (235 g) cake flour
- ½ cup (125 ml) vegetable oil
- 1 tbsp (12 g) baking powder
- 1½ cups (300 g) granulated sugar
- 1 tsp (5 g) salt
- 7 large egg, room temperature
- 1 tbsp (15 ml) vanilla extract
- ½ tsp (2 g) cream of tartar
- ¾ cup (188 ml) cold water

INSTRUCTIONS

1. Preheat the oven to 325°F

2. Filter the flour and baking powder into a different medium sized bowl.

3. Include 150 grams of sugar and salt and rush to consolidate.

4. Using a medium sized bowl, consolidate the egg yolks, water, oil, and vanilla and mix thoroughly.

5. Empty the wet ingredients into the dry ingredients and whisk thoroughly.

6. In a huge bowl, beat the egg whites and cream of tartar with an electric hand mixer until frothy. Continuously include the rest of the sugar and beat until soft peaks appear and the egg whites are lustrous.

7. Empty the egg yolk batter into the egg whites and crease to join with a spatula.

8. Pour the batter into two ungreased 8.5-inch (21 cm) round cake pans. Note that greasing the pans will make it difficult for the cake to rise.

9. Heat in the oven for 40-45 minutes, or until a toothpick embedded in the focal point of the cakes tells the truth (doneness) .

10. Expel the cakes from the oven and chill the cake upside off. When cool to the touch, slide a balance spatula around the edges to discharge the cakes from the pans.

FLOURLESS CAKE

Preparation Time: 10 minutes

Cook Time: 45 minutes

Total Time: 55 minutes

INGREDIENTS

- 6 enormous eggs
- ¾ cup white sugar
- 1 cup unsalted butter
- 18 (1 ounce) squares bittersweet chocolate
- ¼ teaspoon salt
- ½ cup water

INSTRUCTIONS

1. Preheat the oven to 300°F

2. Grease a round cake pan and put aside.

3. Using a saucepan or heat resistant bowl, make a compound of sugar, salt and water and heat to dissolve.

4. Get the chocolate melted and pour it into a mixing bowl.

5. Cut the butter into pieces and beat the butter into the chocolate, 1 piece at once.

6. Beat in the hot sugar-water and gradually beat in the eggs, each in turn.

7. Empty the batter into the readied pan. Have a pan much bigger than the cake pan prepared, put the cake pan in the bigger pan and fill the pan with very hot water most of the way up the sides of the cake pan.

8. Prepare cake in the water shower at 300°F for 45 minutes. The middle will in any case look wet. Chill cake for the time being in the pan. To unmold, plunge the base of the cake pan in high temp water for 10 seconds and turn onto a serving plate.

GENOISE CAKE

Preparation Time: 10 minutes

Cook Time: 35 minutes

Total Time: 45 minutes

INGREDIENTS

- 6 eggs
- 200 g caster sugar
- 160 g plain flour
- 25 g cornflour
- 30 g melted butter
- 625 g fresh raspberries (for decoration)

INSTRUCTIONS

1. Preheat the oven to 300°F

2. Generously grease and line a 21 centimeter round cake pan with baking parchment paper and sprinkle some flour on it.

3. Beat the eggs in a big mixing bowl until it becomes white and frothy.

4. Add the sugar gently and beat until trebled in size.

5. Filter together in a bowl the flour and cornflour and crease in cautiously to the egg blend and ultimately overlay in the dissolved butter.

6. Pour the blend or mixture into the greased cake and bake for 35 minutes or until an inserted toothpick comes out clean.

7. Retrieve cake from the oven, and cool for 10 or more minutes in the pan and then turn out onto a cooling rack and remove the parchment paper.

DEVIL'S FOOD CAKE

Preparation Time: 25 minutes

Cook Time: 30 to 35 minutes

Total Time: 1 hr

INGREDIENTS

- 4 enormous eggs at room temperature
- ¾ cup (64 g) dutch-processed cocoa
- 12 tablespoon (170 g) unsalted margarine at room temperature
- 1¾ cups (347 g) granulated sugar
- ½ cup (340 g) milk at room temperature
- 2 cups (241 g) all-Purpose Flour
- 2 teaspoons baking powder
- 2 teaspoons vanilla concentrate
- ½ teaspoon salt

INSTRUCTIONS

1. Preheat the oven to 350°F.

2. Gently grease and flour two 9 inch round cake pans.

3. Beat together the sugar and salt in an enormous mixing bowl until feathery and light, beating should not be less than 5 minutes.

4. Using another mixing bowl, whisk together the flour, cocoa, and baking powder. On the off chance that lumps remain, filter the blend.

5. Add the eggs to the butter mixture each in turn, beating great after every successive egg.

6. Combine the milk and the vanilla concentrate.

7. Include 33% of the flour blend to the batter, at that point include a large portion of the milk, another third of the flour, the rest of the milk, and the rest of the flour, mixing to consolidate after every expansion.

8. Using a bowl scraper or a rubber spatula, scratch the sides and base of the bowl sporadically all through this procedure.

9. Partition the batter equally between the readied pans.

10. Heat the cake(s) in the oven for 30 to 35 minutes until a cake tester or toothpick embedded into the

middle tells the truth, and the cake starts to pull away from the sides of the pan.

11. Expel the cake(s) from the oven, cool them for 5 to 10 minutes, at that point expel them from their pan to a cooling rack. Allow to cool totally before icing.

RED VELVET CAKE

Preparation Time: 20 minutes

COOK TIME: 35 minutes

TOTAL TIME: 55 minutes

INGREDIENTS

- 3 cups all-purpose flour
- 4 large eggs
- 3 cups granulated sugar
- ½ cup cornstarch
- ½ cup unsweetened cocoa powder
- 1 tablespoon baking soda
- 1½ teaspoons baking powder
- 1½ teaspoons salt
- ½ cup vegetable oil
- 1½ cups buttermilk
- 1¼ cups warm water
- 2 tablespoons red food coloring
- 1 teaspoon vanilla extract
- 1 teaspoon distilled white vinegar

Icing:

- 1 cup butter softened
- 16 ounces cream cheese softened

- 1 teaspoon vanilla extract
- 4 cups powdered sugar

INSTRUCTIONS

1. Preheat the oven to 350°F.

2. Grease three 9-inch round cake pans.

3. Sprinkle with flour and tap out the excesses.

4. Combine flour, sugar, cornstarch, cocoa, baking soda, baking powder, and salt in a stand mixer utilizing a low speed until joined.

5. Include eggs, buttermilk, warm water, vegetable oil, vanilla, vinegar, and food coloring and beat for 2 to 3 minutes on a medium speed until smooth.

6. Evenly distribute the batter among the three arranged baking pans and place inside the oven.

7. Oven heat for 30-35 minutes until the cake passes the toothpick test (stick a toothpick in and it tells the truth).

8. Cool on cooling racks for 15 minutes and afterward turn out the cakes onto the racks and permit to cool totally before icing.

To make the icing.

1. In a huge bowl, beat together butter and cream cheese until soft. Utilize a hand mixer or stand mixer for best outcomes.

2. Include vanilla and beat until well consolidated.

3. Beat in 1 cup of powdered sugar sequentially, until the icing is smooth.

4. Amass and ice the cake which must have cooled completely. Set one layer on a plate with the level side looking up (or, if your cake rose excessively, cut its risen top with a knife to make it level). Equally spread a thick layer of the icing over the cake to the edge. Top with the subsequent cake layer, gather side together and do the same for the last layer. Spread the rest of the icing over the top and sides of the cake.

PUMPKIN CAKE

Preparation Time: 15 minutes

Cook Time: 35 minutes

Total time: 50 minutes

INGREDIENTS

- 15 pumpkin puree
- 3 large eggs
- 1½ cups granulated sugar
- 2 teaspoons baking powder
- 1 teaspoon baking soda
- 1 cup vegetable oil
- 2 teaspoons cinnamon

For the Cream Cheese Icing:

- 8 oz Cream Cheese at room temperature
- 8 tablespoons unsalted butter, room temperature
- 2 teaspoons vanilla extract
- 1 cup powdered sugar

INSTRUCTIONS

1. Preheat the oven to 350°F.

2. Grease and line a 9×13 baking pan.

3. In a large bowl, whisk together flour, sugar, baking soda, baking powder and cinnamon.

4. Using a medium sized bowl, whisk the eggs, vegetable oil and pumpkin until well incorporated.

5. Combine both mixtures and beat to arrive at a smooth batter.

6. Pour the batter into the greased baking pan and bake at 350°F for 35-40 minutes, or until a toothpick inserted in the center comes out clean.

7. Allow the cake to cool completely in the pan before icing.

To Make Cream Cheese Icing:

Put all the icing ingredients in the bowl of a stand mixer and using the whisk attachment, beat from medium to high speed until combined. Remember to scrape the bowl at intervals.

WHITE CAKE

Preparation Time: 10 minutes

Cook Time: 35 minutes

Total Time: 45 minutes

INGREDIENTS

- 2½ cup flour
- ½ cup butter
- 5 egg whites
- 4 teaspoons baking powder
- 1½ cup sugar
- ¾ cup milk
- Powdered sugar
- Shredded coconut

INSTRUCTIONS

1. Preheat the oven to 350°F.

2. Grease and line a 9 inch square pan and set aside.

3. Sift the flour and baking powder together and add milk.

3. Pour the egg whites in a bowl and beat and gradually add the sugar.

5. Cream butter and combine with the egg white mixture.

6. Gradually add the sifted ingredients while ensuring proper beating until smooth.

7. Transfer the mix into the prepared pan, sprinkle with powdered sugar and cover with a light layer of shredded coconut.

8. Bake in the oven for 35 to 40 minutes or until it meets the toothpick test.

9. Allow to cool off for 10 minutes and transfer to a cooling rack for complete cooling.

CAKE ICING

Overview

Icing is the creamy coating used for covering the outside of a cake. It is composed of ingredients like sugar, egg whites, butter, etc. Cake baked in layers can be joined together by icing thereby acting as the filler, but a filler can be made to serve the filling purpose. But it is more economical to use the icing used for covering to do the filling as well.

Icing is used for the purpose of improving the quality (taste and appearance) of a cake and also for keeping the cake moist. A few of them are straightforward, consisting just of powdered sugar blended in with a fluid, while others are increasingly intricate furthermore, including various ingredients.

In decorating cakes, they are first covered with plain white icing and subsequently other icing colors are applied. Unique thoughts and plans may along these lines be worked out in an alluring approach to coordinate a color plan or complete an improving thought. A pastry bag is the most acceptable utensil for this reason. They might be spread over the cake, put on thick in a level way, or masterminded in extravagant plans on a plain foundation of basic icing with the utilization of a pastry bag. These beautifications might be made in white or in different hues to suit the structure chosen for decoration.

You may wonder what cakes might be served without icings and fillings and what ones are improved by these backups. Sponge cakes, when in doubt, are definitely not iced intricately, for an overwhelming icing doesn't orchestrate with the light surface of this sort of cake. In a case where anything is wanted, a straightforward sugar icing is utilized or the outside of the cake is dampened with the white of an egg and afterward sprinkled with sugar.

Butter cakes, particularly when prepared in layers, in spite of the fact that they are frequently a lot more extravagant than sponge cakes, are normally iced. From my own point of view icing isn't a big deal because the sweet cake is of greater priority to consume, the icing though it's sweet but does more of improving the look of the cake. This segment will treat how to prepare icings you can use to complement your cakes.

TYPES OF ICING

1. Uncooked icing

2. Cooked icing

Uncooked icing

In uncooked icings, which are effortlessly made, confectioner's sugar is soaked with a fluid of some sort and afterward enhanced using different manners of flavors.

Butter Icing

Ingredients

- 1 egg white
- 1 tablespoon butter
- 1 tablespoon cream
- 1½ cups powdered sugar
- ½ teaspoon vanilla

Instructions

Cream the butter, include the sugar, weakening it with the cream, and include the vanilla. Beat the egg white and add to the blend, proceeding with the beating until the blend is dry and prepared to spread.

Plain Icing

Ingredients

- 1 egg white
- ½ teaspoon vanilla
- 1¼ cups confectioner's sugar
- 2 teaspoon cold water

Instructions

Beat the egg white until it is firm. Filter in the sugar and include a little bit of the water once in a while until all the water and sugar are included. Beat together completely, include the seasoning, also, and spread on the cake.

Cold-water Icing

Ingredients

- 1 cup confectioner's sugar
- 1 teaspoon lemon juice
- 2 tablespoon cold water

Instructions

Add the sugar to the lemon juice and water, beat together thoroughly, and spread with a knife or spatula on any desired cake.

Chocolate Butter Icing

Ingredients

- 1 oz. chocolate
- 1½ cups powdered sugar
- 1 tablespoon butter
- ½ egg
- 3 tablespoon milk
- Vanilla

Instructions

Cream the butter and include the sugar bit by bit, dampening with the milk and egg to make the blend sufficiently slender to spread. Liquefy the chocolate in a pot over heated water and fill the icing blend. Include the vanilla. Beat completely also, if more sugar or fluid is expected to make the icing thicker or more slender, include until it is suitable enough to spread.

Chocolate Water Icing

Ingredients

- 1 sq. chocolate
- ½ teaspoon vanilla
- 1 ½ cups pounded sugar
- 3 tablespoons bubbling water

Instructions

Soften the chocolate in a twofold kettle, include the bubbling water what's more, the sugar, and mix together until smooth. Include the vanilla. Spread on the cake.

Ornamental Icing

Ingredients

- 3 cups confectioner's sugar
- 3 egg whites
- 3 teaspoons lemon juice

Instructions

Put the egg whites into a bowl, include a tad bit of the sugar, and beat. Keep including sugar until the blend turns out to be as thick to beat well, and afterward include the lemon juice. Include the rest of the sugar, and keep beating until the icing is sufficiently thick to spread. Spread a far layer over the cake furthermore, permit it to solidify. At the point when this is dry, spread it with another layer to make a smooth surface, and add more sugar to the remaining icing until it is of an extremely solid consistency. Shade and flavor as wanted, place in a pastry bag, and power through pastry tips to make any ideal designs.

Orange Icing

Ingredients

- 1 ½ cups confectioner's sugar
- 4 tablespoons squeezed orange
- Few drops orange concentrate
- Orange shading for coloring

Instructions

Filter the sugar into the squeezed orange and beat completely. Include the orange concentrate and only a little bit of the orange shading for an even color. Spread on the cake.

Cooked Icing

Cooked icings are made by beating a hot sugar syrup into very much beaten egg whites. In the wake of being flavored, icings of this sort might be utilized without the inclusion of other fixings/ingredients or they might be joined with organic products, nuts, coconut, and so forth.

Due to the nature of cooked icings they must be quickly applied to the cake as soon as possible using a spatula or knife. If after applying the icing, there's roughness and the surface is not smooth enough a hot knife can be used on the surface in a cold state. This will improve the smoothness and appearance.

Earthy Colored Sugar Boiled Icing

Ingredients

- 1¼ cups brown/earthy colored sugar
- ¼ cup white sugar
- 2 egg whites
- Pinch of cream of tartar
- ⅓ cup water

Instructions

Heat up the sugar and the water until it strings or structures a hard ball when attempted in chilly water. Beat the egg whites until solid, including a touch of cream of tartar while beating. Pour the hot syrup over the egg whites. What's more, keep beating.

Flavor with vanilla whenever wanted. Beat until sufficiently solid to spread.

Efficient or Time Saving Icing

Ingredients

- 1 egg white
- ⅞ cup granulated sugar
- 3 tablespoons water

Instructions

Put the sugar, water, and egg white into the upper piece of a little twofold heater. Have the water in the lower part bubbling quickly. Set the part containing the ingredients set up and beat continually for 7 minutes with a rotating egg mixer, until a cooked icing that will stay set up will be prepared for use. The water in the lower container must bubble quickly all through the 7 minutes.

Caramel Icing

Ingredients

- ½ cup earthy/brown colored sugar
- ½ tablespoon butter
- ¾ cup milk

Instructions

Heat up the ingredients together until a delicate ball is shaped when the blend is attempted in cool water. Cool and beat until of the right consistency to spread. Spread this icing rather far. On the off chance, cleaved nuts might be added to it while it is being beaten.

Maple Icing

Ingredients

- ½ cup maple sugar
- ½ tablespoon butter
- ¾ cup milk

Instructions

Heat up the ingredients together until a delicate ball is shaped when the blend is attempted in cool water. Cool and beat until of the right consistency to spread.

Boiling Icing

Ingredients

- 1 egg white
- 1 cup sugar

- ½ cup water
- Pinch of cream of tartar

Instructions

Put the sugar and water to cook in a pan. Bubble until a genuinely hard ball is shaped when the syrup is attempted in cool water or then again until it strings when dropped from a spoon. In the event that a thermometer is utilized to test the syrup, it ought to register 240 to 242 degrees Fahrenheit when the syrup is taken from the oven. Beat the egg white, include the cream of tartar, and keep beating until the egg white is hardened. At that point, pour the hot syrup over the beaten egg white gradually, so as not to cook the egg, beating quickly until all the syrup has been included. Keep on beating with a spoon or egg whip until the icing is light and practically hardened enough to spread on the cake. At that point place the bowl over a vessel containing bubbling water, and beat for 3 or 4 minutes while the water bubbles quickly underneath. With this treatment, the icing won't change in consistency, however will get simpler to deal with and will allow it to be utilized for a more drawn out time frame without turning out to be hard.

MEASUREMENTS AND CONVERSIONS

STANDARD MEASUREMENTS

MASS	METRIC EQUIVALENTS (g)
ounce	28 g
4 ounces or 1/4 pound	113 g
1/3 pound	150 g
8 ounces or 1/2 pound	230 g
2/3 pound	300 g
12 ounces or 3/4 pound	340 g
1 pound or 16 ounces	450 g
2 pounds	900 g

LIQUID MEASUREMENTS

QUANTITY	METRIC EQUIVALENT
1 teaspoon	5 ml
1 tablespoon (1/2 fluid ounce)	15 ml
1 fluid ounce (1/8 cup)	30 ml
1/4 cup (2 fluid ounces)	60 ml
1/3 cup	80 ml
1/2 cup (4 fluid ounces)	120 ml
2/3 cup	160 ml
3/4 cup (6 fluid ounces)	180 ml
1 cup (8 fluid ounces) (half a pint)	240 ml
1 1/2 cups (12 fluid ounces)	350 ml

2 cups (1 pint) (16 fluid ounces)	475 ml
3 cups (1 1/2 pints)	700 ml
4 cups (2 pints) (1 quart)	950 ml
4 quarts (1 gallon)	3.8 L

NON LIQUID MEASUREMENTS

⅛ teaspoon	0.5 ml
¼ teaspoon	1.5 ml
½ teaspoon	2 ml
¾ teaspoon	4 ml
1 teaspoon	5 ml
1 tablespoon (½ ounce)	15 ml
2 tablespoon (1 ounce)	30 ml
¼ cup (2 ounces)	60 ml
⅓ cup	75 ml

½ cup (4 ounces)	125 ml
⅔ cup	150 ml
¾ cup (6 ounces)	175 ml
1 cup (8 ounces)	250 ml
2 cups	500 ml
3 cups	750 ml
4 cups (32 ounces)	1 L

OVEN TEMPERATURES

Degree Fahrenheit	Degree Celsius
275° F	140° C
300° F	150° C
325° F	165° C
350° F	180° C
375° F	190° C
400° F	200° C

425° F	220° C

Note:

1 stick of butter equals 4 ounces (113 g).

Printed in Great Britain
by Amazon

25539026R00066